CHESTER STRING SERIES

for Viola and Piano

Edited and arranged by
PEGGY RADMALL

BOOK 2 (1st to 3rd position)

			page
1.	Nobodye's Gigge	Richard Farnaby	1
2.	Bonny Sweet Robin	Giles Farnaby	3
3.	Aire Round O	John Eccles	5
4.	Minuet	John Eccles	6
5.	Trumpet Aire	John Eccles	7
6.	Jigg	John Eccles	8
7.	Scotch Tune	Henry Purcell	9
8.	Dance	Henry Purcell	11
9.	Arietta	Pergolesi	13
10.	Two Serenade Movements	G. B. Viotti	15
11.	Two Miniatures	Stephen Heller	23

Extra Viola Parts Available

CHESTER MUSIC
part of The Music Sales Group
14-15 Berners Street, London W1T 3LJ, UK

WARNING: The photocopying of any pages of this publication is illegal. If copies are made in breach of copyright, the Publishers will, where possible, sue for damages.

Every illegal copy means a lost sale. Lost sales lead to shorter print runs and rising prices. Soon the music goes out of print, and more fine works are lost from the repertoire.

NOBODYE'S GIGGE

RICHARD FARNABY

© Copyright 1952, 1991 for all Countries
Chester Music Ltd. 14–15 Berners Street, London, W1T 3LJ

CH00399

All rights reserved
Printed in England

BONNY SWEET ROBIN

GILES FARNABY
(1560-1600)

A SET OF AIRES AND DANCES

1 AIRE ROUND O

JOHN ECCLES
(1650-1735)

2 MINUET

3 TRUMPET AIRE

Allegro moderato

4 JIGG

SCOTCH TUNE

H. PURCELL
(1659-1695)

© Copyright 1952, 1991 for all Countries
Chester Music Ltd. 14–15 Berners Street, London, W1T 3LJ

10

DANCE

H. PURCELL

ARIETTA

PERGOLESI
(1710-1786)

TWO SERENADE MOVEMENTS

1
PASTORALE

G. B. VIOTTI
(1753-1824)

rit.
p
p
attacca

2

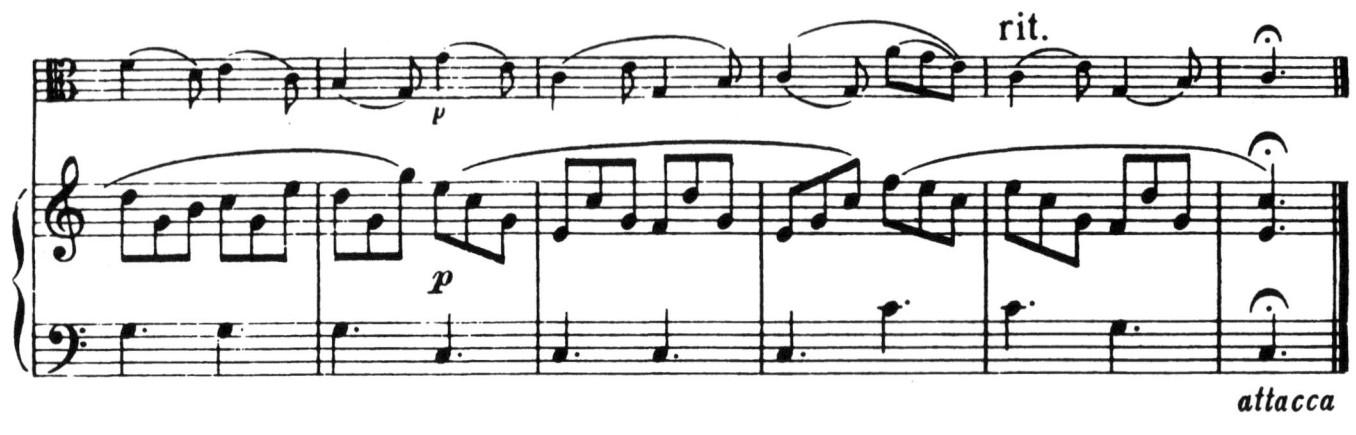

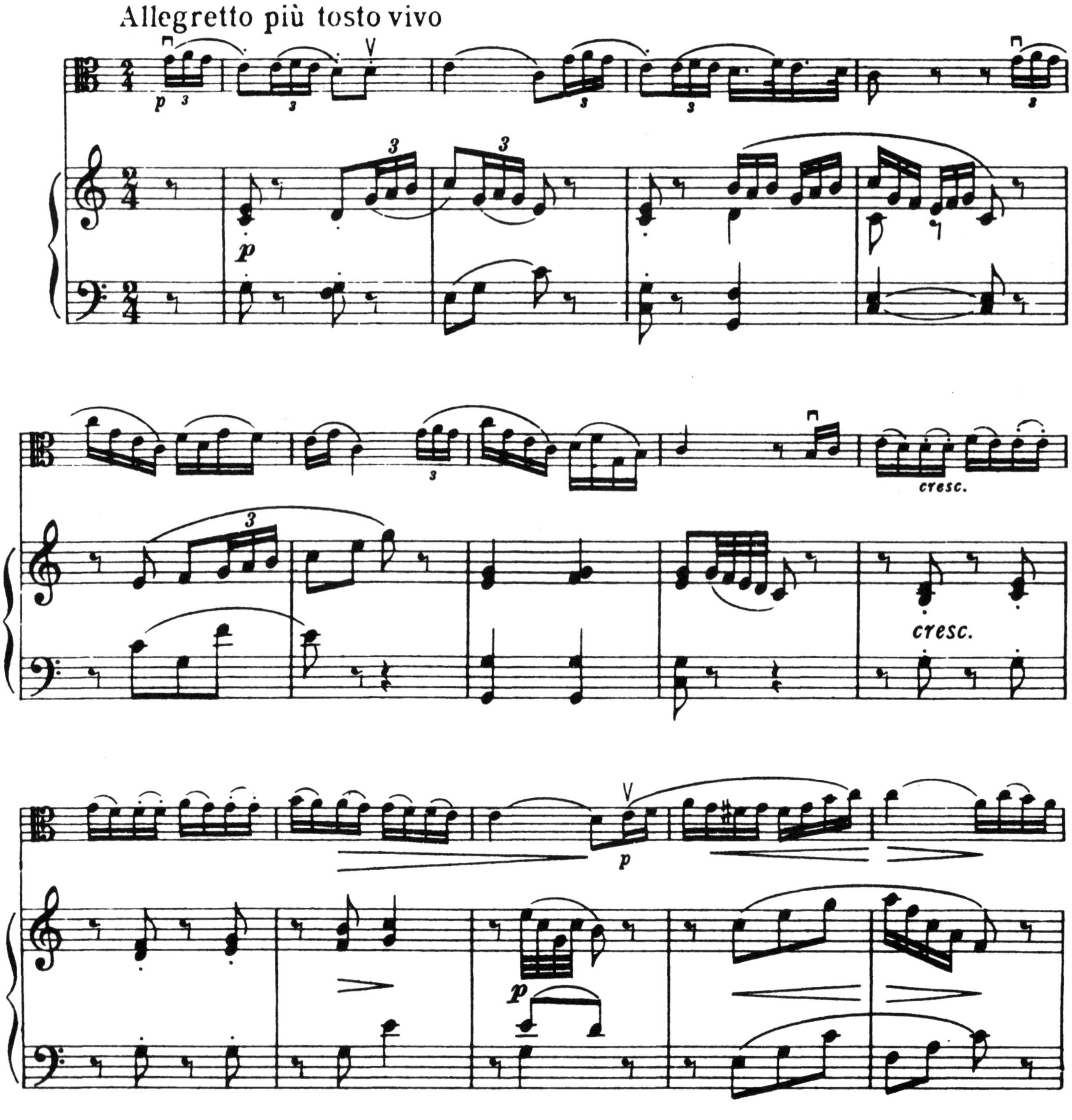
Allegretto più tosto vivo
p
p
cresc.
cresc.
p
p

19

22

TWO MINIATURES

I

STEPHEN HELLER
(1814-88)

© Copyright 1959, 1991 for all Countries
Chester Music Ltd. 14–15 Berners Street, London, W1T 3LJ

II

Allegro vivace

poco meno mosso

26